WILDFLOWERS
OF AMERICA

Text and captions
Adrian Davies

Photography
Bruce Coleman Ltd

Design
Teddy Hartshorn

Editorial
Trevor Hall
Andrew Preston
Pauline Graham
Fleur Robertson
Gill Waugh

Production
Gerald Hughes
Ruth Arthur

Publishing Director
David Gibbon

CLB 2226
© 1989 Colour Library Books Ltd, Godalming, Surrey, England.
© Illustrations 1989 Bruce Coleman Ltd, Uxbridge, Middlesex, England.
All rights reserved.
Color separations by Hong Kong Graphic Arts Ltd, Hong Kong.
This 1989 edition published by Arch Cape Press, a division of dilithium Press, Ltd,
distributed by Crown Publishers, Inc, 225 Park Avenue South, New York, New York 10003.
Printed and bound in Hong Kong.
Davies, Adrian.
Wildflowers of America.
1. Wild flowers – United States Identifi-
cation. 2. Wild flowers – United States
– Pictorial works. I. Title. II Title:
Wild flowers of America.
QK115.D 1989 582.13'0973 88-35129
ISBN 0-517-68242-7
h g f e d c b a

WILDFLOWERS
OF AMERICA

Adrian Davies

ARCH CAPE PRESS
NEW YORK

America is a huge country, the fourth largest in the world after the USSR, Canada and China. Including Alaska, it covers an area of over 3,500,000 square miles. At its widest point it extends for some 3,000 miles from east to west, and about 1,500 miles from north to south, thus covering a large latitudinal range. It is a land of extremes, ranging between hot, dry deserts, bleak, snow-covered mountain tops and steamy swamps.

Such a diversity of climates and habitats has encouraged an incredible array of wild flowers, trees and other plants. There are many thousands of flowers – California alone has over 4,000 species from about 750 genera. About forty-five percent of those are endemic – in other words occurring naturally in this region!

Many of America's flowers are common and familiar, whilst others are more difficult to find, requiring careful searching, often in remote locations. Some are carnivorous, such as the insectivorous plants which ensnare small insects for essential nutrients otherwise lacking in their habitat. Others have evolved special relationships with animals to ensure that pollination takes place. The fascinating yuccas of the southwestern deserts are pollinated only by a small moth, for example, whilst many red and orange flowers rely on hummingbirds to carry the pollen from one plant to another.

Over the centuries many plants have been used by man for medicine, food and herbs, as well as for clothing, either using the plant fibres to spin into yarn, or their juice as dye for cloth. The native Indians in particular had a use for most of the plants that grew around them, and today many of our modern medicines are derived from plants. The early European settlers brought plants such as chicory with them, and these often now grow wild in the landscape alongside the native plants. The settlers changed the American landscape greatly, bringing huge areas of native grassland into cultivation, and frequently taking many native plants to the verge of extinction in the process.

The distribution of America's wild flowers is dependent primarily on the physical factors of geology, which governs the topography or physical structure of the landscape and its soil type, and the prevailing climate.

Simplistically, America can be thought of as two chains of mountains running from north to south on either side of a vast area of lowland. This lowland region occupies over a half of the area of the country, whilst the western region of mountains occupies nearly a third. But this is, of course, a gross over-simplification that fails to take into account the infinite variety of plains, plateaus, mountains and valleys in this vast country.

The mountain system running from north to south through much of the eastern part of the country is the Appalachian, a range of relatively low mountains rarely exceeding 6,000 feet. They are by far the oldest mountains in America, having been uplifted some 200 to 300 million years ago. They begin in Maine and extend down to central Alabama. The heavily glaciated Adirondack Mountains of New England are composed of some of the oldest rocks on earth, whilst the greatest heights are achieved in the Blue Ridge and Great Smoky Mountains of North Carolina – Mount Mitchell is the highest peak here, at 6,684 feet.

Due to their relatively low height, the Appalachians are home to only a limited number of true alpine plants. The western ranges of mountains have much higher elevations and consequently have a correspondingly higher number of alpine plants. The Rocky Mountains have over 300 flowering plants found at and above the timberline.

The American Rockies are part of a huge chain of mountains that form a spine throughout the Americas, starting in Alaska and running south through Canada and the United States to join up with the great Andean range of South America. They are altogether a much more substantial range of mountains than the Appalachians: even the lowest passes through the Rockies are higher than the peaks of the Appalachians, and there are forty-five peaks exceeding 14,000 feet. Mount Elbert, in Colorado, is the highest point in the American Rockies, at 14,433 feet.

Consisting of a number of discontinuous ranges, the Rockies are geologically very complex. Mountain glaciers, some of which are still in existence, have sculpted the higher peaks, giving them a serrated appearance, whilst the valley heads are often shaped like huge amphitheatres. Most valleys are narrow and steep-sided. The snows and glaciers of the Rockies have given rise to six major rivers in North America, including the Missouri, Snake, Colorado and Rio Grande.

Between the Rockies and the mountains of the Pacific coast lies a vast region of high plateaus and isolated mountain ranges. It is generally a semi-arid region, and very sparsely populated. Nearly half of the area is a land of interior drainage, where streams do not run into the sea, but instead drain into brackish lakes or desert sinks. This intermontane region is known as the Great Basin.

To the north, a vast lava plateau is drained by the Columbia River and its main tributary the Snake, which has cut a mile-deep gorge known as Hell's Canyon through the underlying rocks.

To the south, the Colorado River has cut a similar gorge through the sedimentary rocks of the Colorado Plateau to form the spectacular Grand Canyon – the deepest cleft in the surface of the earth. The land here is very dry, and only isolated juniper trees and spindly scrub can grow. To the west lies Death Valley, one of the most forbidding places on earth. Lying some 280 feet below sea level, it is the lowest point in the western hemisphere. An air temperature of 134°F has been recorded here – the hottest ever in North America – while perhaps only two inches of rain will fall in a year. Despite these extremes, many plants and animals do manage to live in this hostile environment.

West of the Great Basin, flanking the Pacific coast for almost the entire length of the country, lie the mountains of the Pacific Rim. These are two sets of mountain ranges running parallel down the western side of the country. The range immediately adjacent to the Great Basin is the Sierra Nevada, which continues northwards into the Cascade Range of Washington State. These mountains have steep eastern-facing slopes, with gentler slopes facing the Pacific. Glaciers have carved the more southerly regions into a series of jagged peaks, which include Mount Whitney in California. At 14,494 feet this mountain is the highest point in the United States outside Alaska. The Cascades are a rugged range surmounted by a series of great volcanoes, many over 10,000 feet high. Several have erupted in historical times, such as Lassen Peak in 1915, and most recently Mount St. Helens, which erupted in 1980 with such force that full-grown Douglas Fir trees some twenty miles away were flattened by the blast!

The ranges adjacent to the coast are generally of lower elevation, with Mount Olympus in Washington State reaching 7,865 feet, and Thompson Peak in the Klamath Mountains of northern California reaching over 9,000 feet.

Between the two mountain regions of the east and west lies a vast expanse of lowland, the agricultural heartland of America. The region occupies over half of the area of north America, extending west from New York State to the Rockies, and northward from Texas to Canada. Indeed the region continues into Canada, forming the great prairies and grasslands of Alberta, Saskatchewan and Manitoba. This entire region is of low relief, broken only locally by low masses of hills and small mountains. The northeastern part of the region was heavily glaciated during the Ice Ages, leaving a whole series of lakes in Michigan, Minnesota and Wisconsin. Iowa, Illinois, Indiana and Ohio have a gently undulating relief underlain by fertile glacial soils. The majority of the region is drained by the great Mississippi River and its tributaries.

The final major physical region to consider is the Atlantic Coastal Plain, a flat, low-lying plain stretching from Cape Cod and Long Island to Florida, where large areas are poorly drained, culminating in the great swamps of the Everglades. The plain is dissected by many bays and estuaries which form a very irregular coastline. The Atlantic Plain merges with the Gulf Coastal Plain, and continues round into Mexico.

The other major factor influencing the distribution of plant life is the climate. As with the physical structure, generalizations regarding the climate of a particular region can be misleading – individual hills or valleys can greatly influence the climate within a small area, perhaps creating rain shadows or frost pockets, for example. As might be expected from its size and varied topography, America has a wide range of climatic types, from the near Arctic conditions of the western mountain summits, to the humid, sub-tropical climate of the southeast.

The eastern half of the country east of the 100th meridian tends to be wetter than the west, the division being the Great Plains which adjoin the eastern slopes of the Rocky Mountains. Rainfall averages from thirty to forty inches per annum in the more northerly areas, while up to sixty inches is more normal further south in those states bordering the Gulf of Mexico. There is no significant landmass to substantially alter air movements between the Gulf of Mexico and the Arctic Ocean. As a result, the vast Mississippi valley is a land of climatic extremes and high winds. Southerly winds carry warm air from the Gulf of Mexico hundreds of miles inland, whilst northerly winds often bring bitterly cold conditions as far south as Texas or Florida.

Much of the southeast has very high humidity both day and night, and frequent thunderstorms. Temperatures are usually high in summer, averaging between 85-104°F, dropping perhaps only to 70°F or so at night. In winter warm, moist maritime tropical air alternates with cold air from the north. Temperatures may be between 50-60°F for much of the time, tplummetingto many degrees below freezing during the invasions of cold winds from the north.

Across the southern Midwestern and Middle Atlantic states lies the corn belt, which endures hot summers and long, cold winters. Between thirty to fifty inches of precipitation may fall in a year, mostly as snow.

Further north, in a region surrounding the Great Lakes, summers tend to be cooler – though still humid – but winters are very cold due to the continental polar airstream from the north. Temperatures may average only 32°F or less in winter, and snow is frequent and heavy. The growing season is from 70-150 days, much shorter than the 150-200 days further south.

The climate of the western half of the country is highly complex. The vast area of plateaus and basins extending from the mountains of the Cascades and Sierra Nevada to the Rockies is arid, with very low precipitation, less than ten inches in Arizona, Nevada and Utah and less than twenty inches in the rest of the region. The mountains intercept some moisture-laden winds off the Pacific and may have twenty-five to thirty inches per year, often falling as snow. This melts in summer and provides water for the irrigation of the region's summer crops. Temperatures in the desert areas may be very high, reaching well over 100°F during the day and falling sharply at night – conditions to which desert plants are well adapted.

With low temperatures all year round, the higher peaks of the Rockies and other mountain ranges experience a climate similar to that of the tundra and Arctic regions of Alaska and Canada. Here, temperatures may reach a maximum of perhaps only 50°F in summer, falling far below zero in winter. Precipitation can be very high, mostly in the form of snow.

West of the Sierra Nevada and Cascade Mountains lies a coastal belt influenced by the warm, moist air from the Pacific. Here winters are generally mild and wet, most areas receiving between thirty and forty inches of rain per year, though the extreme south is much drier. There is much regional variation – the Olympic Mountains in Washington State can receive over 135 inches per year, the highest rainfall in mainland America! The mild, damp climate has favored the development of lush forests in this region, usually of Douglas fir, hemlock, cedar and the giant redwoods, many of which exceed 300 feet in height.

The complex relationship between the climate and physical structure of America has led to the formation of several distinct habitats in which native wild flowers grow. Ignoring Alaska, these are, broadly speaking, the Arctic-alpine regions of the high western mountain ranges, the forests and woodlands, the dry deserts, the grasslands and prairies, and the varied wetlands, marshes and coastal regions. Many flowers are very specific in their habitat preference – cacti are only found in the arid desert areas for example, whilst most of the insectivorous plants are only to be found in constantly-waterlogged bogs and swamps. Others, however, are more widespread, being found in most habitats throughout the country.

In habitats with the harshest or most extreme conditions, plants are found with specific adaptations to those conditions. As we have seen, the alpine environment is often severe, with biting winds for much of the year draining the moisture from plants, and periods of drought and baking heat often followed by heavy rain! The plants which survive and even flourish here all have various adaptations to cope with these harsh conditions.

The alpine zone of mountains lies between the "timber-line", the limit of tree growth, and the zone of permanent snow, where most plant life is absent. In the Rockies, alpine plants start to appear at between 6,000 and 8,000 feet and thus relatively few are found in the eastern mountain ranges of the Appalachians, where altitudes are generally much lower.

Perhaps the most noticeable characteristic of true alpine plants is their low height, usually coupled with small, tight cushions of closely-matted stalks. The purple saxifrage is a good example. This plant's domed shape cuts down wind resistance and acts as a heat trap. Measurements taken from within typical cushions have shown that it may be up to 60°F warmer within the cushion than in the surrounding air. This heat can be retained for many hours, helping to counter the great day to night fluctuations in temperature experienced in these regions. The leaves and stems are often dark colored to absorb heat, and are usually covered in dense hairs to reduce desiccation. Many of the plants have a rich, viscous cell sap which acts like anti-freeze, protecting the tissues from frost damage. The plants themselves must be supple to withstand the fierce winds – a rigid, woody stem would snap. Those woody plants that do grow here, such as the Rocky Mountain snow willow, grow along the surface of the ground, rising to just a few inches above it.

Another way in which heat is trapped by these plants is by the flowers themselves, which are often parabolic-shaped. These concentrate the rays of the sun and may actually track the sun, rotating their stems so that they always point towards it. Alpine poppies and mountain avens are good examples of this phenomenon, known as heliotropism. By warming the central part of the flower in this way insect pollinators are attracted, while raising the temperature of the stigma within the flower helps to speed up the germination of the pollen grains.

With such a short growing season there is hardly time for flowers to bloom and set seed. Even though some buttercups have been known to produce flowers just five days after the snow around them has melted, and seeds just seventeen days later, there is still no time for the seed to mature and produce seeds of its own. Thus most alpines are perennials – in the Rocky Mountains, of the 300 or so species of flowering plant found above the timberline, only two are annuals, one of which produces flowers the size of pinheads! Many plants take years to build up sufficient reserves to flower. A mat of moss campion may take ten years to produce its first flower, and another ten before the whole plant is able to bloom. The growth rate of most alpines is very slow – a mat of mountain avens three feet across could well be a hundred years old or more. Glacier lilies take seven years to produce their first flowers, and can die if their leaves are damaged during that time.

Perhaps surprisingly, once the flowers do bloom many are brightly colored, such as the deep blue gentians, the yellow buttercups or the purple saxifrages. These colors not only trap heat but also entice insect pollinators. Many of the insects found in these regions are wingless and live within the sheltered surroundings of plant cushions. They pollinate the plant as they crawl around inside. There are not a great number of insect pollinators, so many flowers are wind-pollinated or self-fertilizing. Some buttercups, for example, can set seed without being fertilized. Some of the saxifrages, such as Merten's saxifrage, form small bulbils instead of flowers, which drop to the ground, winter beneath the snow, and produce new plants the following spring. Other plants overwinter as well-developed flower buds, ready to bloom as soon as the growing season arrives. Most alpines use the wind as the main agent for seed dispersal, and have light seeds and fruits, often with long, feathery plumes easily wafted by the wind.

As so much of the plant's energy is taken up with the building of food reserves, it is not surprising that many alpines have extensive root systems, enabling them to tap water from a wide area, as well as providing the plant with a good, solid anchorage against the wind. Plants just a few inches high can have roots three or more feet in length.

Many alpines grow in rock crevices, their roots penetrating the finest of cracks. Here they gain shelter from the wind and grazing animals. They often appear to be splitting the rock, and the name "saxifrage" is derived from the Latin meaning "rockbreaker." They tend to have a rosette formation of leaves at their base, arranged so that each leaf receives as much sunlight as possible.

Away from the mountain tops, but still at high elevations above the timberline, are extensive areas of meadowland. With the arrival of spring these produce one of the finest floral displays to be seen anywhere in the world. Even before the snow has finally gone, great drifts of avalanche, or glacier lilies appear, carpeting the ground with their beautiful white and golden flowers. Mountain Pasque flowers appear early too (the word "Pasque" is an old French word for Easter), often flowering under a blanket of snow. Within just a few days of warmer weather the meadows are ablaze with a myriad flowers, all blooming simultaneously to take advantage of the short growing season. Paintbrushes, owl's clover, penstemon, shooting stars and harebells are just a few of the many plants which cover acre upon acre in a dense mass of flowers, producing a riot of color. The spectacle does not last long though, as the flowering season is short at these altitudes, but a visit to an alpine flower meadow in spring is a "must" for anyone interested in wild flowers.

In the same way that the plants of the high mountains show adaptations to their hostile environment, so too the plants of the desert regions – often in spectacular ways. Strictly speaking, the word "desert" implies a land that is devoid of life. Better terms to use for the dry regions of the west are semi-desert or arid regions. However, as the word desert is so frequently used, its use will be continued here. Contrary to popular belief, these regions support a wealth of plant and animal life.

Broadly speaking, there are two main types of desert in the western United States. Firstly, there is the vast region of the Great Basin, known as sagebrush desert. It is generally cooler than the more southerly regions, and is sparsely covered with deciduous perennial woody plants that possess small, silvery leaves. Sagebrush is the most characteristic plant, but others such as rabbitbrush and hopsage are common. Common flowers here include desert primroses, stickleaf and several species of yucca.

South of the sagebrush-dominated desert lies a hotter, drier region, extending from southwest Arizona, through New Mexico and into southwest Texas. Botanically, it is dominated by the creosote bush. This remarkable plant is very efficient at collecting water from the arid environment. It has a far-reaching network of rootlets which penetrate the gravelly soil so efficiently that all available water is collected. This will usually be derived from dew, so each creosote bush needs a large area of ground to sustain it. Once established, it gathers water so thoroughly that no other plants can grow within several yards of it. This will apply not only to other species but also to its own seedlings. Thus very few seeds are produced. Instead, the bush sends out new stems from its base which draw on the slowly-expanding network of roots. As the bush spreads outwards the stems in the middle tend to die off, and the whole plant expands in the shape of a ring. These rings often become very large, up to eighty feet across, and, whilst the individual stems themselves are not particularly old, if the plant is considered as a whole, it may have been growing on the same site for over 10,000 years, making the creosote bush the oldest living organism in the world!

Probably the most familiar group of plants in this region are the cacti, which grow here in abundance. There are some 2,000 different species, all of which live naturally only in the Americas. The majority are succulent plants (from the Latin *succus,* meaning juice), having fleshy, swollen stems (and occasionally leaves) which retain a store of water, as well as also being green and carrying out the process of photosynthesis. Cacti are xerophytic plants; that is, they are naturally adapted to life in dry habitats, achieved primarily by having a very low water loss during the process of photosynthesis.

Photosynthesis is a remarkable process that relies on two basic components: water and carbon dioxide. In the case of normal land plants, water is obtained through the roots, whilst carbon dioxide enters through pores in the stems and leaves called stomata. Whenever the stomata open to take in carbon dioxide, water vapour escapes by evaporation. In the case of cacti and other succulent plants, the stomata are shielded from draughts by being situated at the bottom of a groove, and only open at night, keeping water loss due to evaporation down to a minimum. This, however, leads to the problem of carbon dioxide, which would normally be converted into sugars by the action of sunlight, having to be stored in the plant cells in the form of organic acids. As the night goes on, the cell sap becomes increasingly acidic. With the coming of a new day the stomata close again, and the plant starts to turn the stored acids into the sugars that the plant requires. Gradually, throughout the day, the acidity of the plant returns to normal. This process is known as crassulacean acid metabolism, a very cumbersome name for an excellent solution to the problem.

In order to retain large amounts of water within the swollen stems, cacti have large quantities of mucilages – slimy substances within the plant cells which act like a sponge. By this means cacti are able to withstand long periods of drought, during which time they may appear quite lifeless. A laboratory-kept specimen was not watered for six years and still had lost only a third of the original amount of water present in its cells! A giant saguaro, which grows up to sixty-five feet, can take in a ton of water in a single day in the right conditions. A full-grown specimen can weigh up to ten tons, nine of which will be water. The characteristic barrel and finger shapes have evolved as the best for storing the maximum amount of water, with the minimum of surface area exposed to the sun. The thick skin is often ribbed, enabling the plant to shrink in dry periods. By doing so it can withstand the loss of as much as one third of its total weight. Growth is very slow. It may take seventy-five years for a saguaro to produce its first branch, and it may be 250 years old when it achieves its full height. During that time it may have produced some 20 million seeds!

The roots of cacti also show adaptations to the arid conditions. They are generally far-reaching and close to the surface, enabling them to take up any water available in the form of dew as well as rain. Many cacti have bulbous roots that may be larger than the stem above ground. These act as underground water stores. Tall, columnar species may have perpendicular roots which act as stabilizers for the tall plant.

Apart from their shapes and succulence, cacti are noted for their spines, which mainly serve as protection from grazing desert animals. These would find the juicy stems most welcome, although the sap of some cacti, such as the saguaro, does contain a poison. Recent studies have shown that in some species the spines are able to absorb water, though this is probably a minor function. Also, it is likely that the spines break up the flow of air around the plant, so it is always surrounded by still air. The spines, which are actually modified leaves, vary greatly, from fearsome four-inch-long needles to little more than soft hairs.

Cacti do, of course, produce beautiful flowers, often in abundance and in a whole range of colors, except for bright blue. They may be tiny, or up to fifteen inches across. During the day these flowers attract insect pollinators and occasionally hummingbirds, which are attracted to the red and orange flowers. Saguaros bloom throughout May, and are pollinated by long-nosed bats and white-winged doves. The bats, unusually, sip the nectar, whilst the doves carry pollen from flower to flower on their heads. At night other species with white flowers bloom, attracting moths and bats with a range of scents. Cactus flowers are usually solitary blooms, but they can still make a lovely display as they encircle, or even cover the whole surface of the plant.

Following pollination a fruit is formed, which can be minute or as large as an egg. The seeds are held within the fruit pulp. Many are dispersed by birds which eat the fruit, the seeds passing unharmed through the gut, whilst those of ground cacti are dispersed by ants. Most cacti have the ability to reproduce vegetatively as well, small pieces breaking off from the parent plant – usually from the crown – and growing into new plants.

Man has long used cacti for various purposes. The fruits of many species are edible, and are eaten by native Indians, who also derived many hallucinatory substances as well as medicines from them. The large-flowered queen of the night cactus yields a juice containing a glycoside chemical used in the treatment of heart disease.

Cacti are an integral part of the desert ecosystem, providing shelter for many animals and birds. A giant saguaro, for instance, may have snakes, woodpeckers, elf owls and screech owls nesting in holes in its stem.

Another fascinating group of plants to be found in the sagebrush desert are many species of yucca. These are tall plants with rigid, spiny leaves that usually have very sharp points. Those species with broad leaves are often called Spanish daggers. There are a great number of species and identification is often difficult. Many, such as the Joshua tree, so called by the Mormons because when mature it looks like a man holding up his arms to God, grow to fifteen feet or more. All yuccas produce a mass of creamy-white flowers, often making a spectacular display on the bleak, brushy slopes. They are members of the lily family, and so all parts of the flowers, the petals, sepals, anthers and carpels, are arranged in whorls of three.

These flowers are only pollinated by a tiny moth, *Tegeticula yuccasella*, the yucca moth, and the two have evolved a highly specialized and specific relationship which benefits them both. The female moth scrapes pollen from the stamens of a creamy, heavily-scented flower at night and rolls it into a ball, carrying it to another flower in a specially-adapted mouth. She makes a careful inspection of the next flower and, if the ovary is ripe, bores a hole into it and lays an egg. She then climbs up to the stigmas, which form a tube, and pushes the pollen ball into the tubular structure. This ensures fertilization and development of the seeds. The growing moth larvae feed on the developing seeds, but eat only about twenty percent of them. When fully grown, the larvae gnaw their way through the ovary wall and fall to the ground, where they pupate just under the surface. They remain there for about a year until the adult moth emerges. Unpollinated flowers die quickly.

Such specific relationships between plants and insects are rare. Where yuccas are grown outside their normal range, such as in the West Indies, they do not produce seeds as there are no yucca moths to aid pollination.

Native Indians of these regions have long used the flowers and fruits of yuccas for food. Young flower buds contain large amounts of sugar, and the baked fruits of some species taste very much like sweet potatoes. The flowers of some are still eaten by Mexican Indians in such quantities that few plants set mature seed. The tough fibres obtained from yuccas have long been used for making clothing, rope and shoes.

Like the giant cacti, yuccas often play host to a range of animals and birds. A mature Joshua tree may have a pair of Scott's orioles nesting among the leaves, perhaps a woodpecker or elf owl in a hole in the trunk, as well as various insects, which in turn attract mammals and reptiles.

Of course there are many more flowers to be found in these arid regions. Their seeds may lie dormant in the ground for months, even years, waiting for sufficient rain to fall to enable them to sprout leaves and flower. A shower of rain can transform seemingly barren ground into a vast carpet of wild flowers within days, all the plants blooming quickly to take advantage of the moisture before it disappears. These ephemeral plants may be annuals blooming every year, or others whose seeds require a very precise trigger in order for them to risk blooming. If they were to sprout with the first flush of moisture, this may be too soon – there may not be enough rain to sustain their growth. Many wait for a precise combination of triggers before germinating.

Flowers such as desert sand verbena, desert primrose, desert poppy, rock-nettle and yellow bee plant may bloom in such profusion that the whole landscape for many miles is a mass of floral color. For a short while these arid lands are as colorful as any habitat on earth, teeming with insects. But all too soon the spectacle ends as the moisture disappears and, within a few short weeks, the slopes and plains revert to their normal dry and rocky appearance.

Throughout the world, vast areas of fertile, flat land are naturally covered in grass. Europe, Asia, Africa, South and North America all have natural grasslands which, in total, cover a quarter of the land surface of the earth. The North American grasslands are, or were, possibly the greatest and richest of them all.

The natural grasslands of North America cover an area some 1,800 miles long, from the Gulf of Mexico to Canada, right up to the edge of the great Boreal forest, and over 600 miles wide, from the eastern edge of the Rockies across to the edge of the deciduous forests of the east. Before the arrival of European settlers natural grassland accounted for about a third of the vegetation cover of the mainland United States. The land is generally flat, has excellent fertile soils and an equable climate – a combination that makes it highly attractive for cultivation. Vast areas were destroyed to make way for agriculture, and little of the natural vegetation remains. Huge herds of bison and pronghorn antelope once roamed the plains, but were hunted almost to extinction during the 19th century. (Both are now protected, and the pronghorn has made an excellent recovery.) Other typical animals and birds, such as prairie dogs, which once lived in vast "townships" often numbering many thousands of individuals, and prairie grouse, are now only present in small, isolated populations.

The original grasslands consisted of three main zones, each characterized by different grasses. In the eastern section of the region rainfall is plentiful, up to forty inches per anum, and soils are good. This was the true prairie, where grasses grew high enough to conceal a man on horseback. Typical species were Indian grass, big and little bluestem and prairie cord grass, though as many as eighty different species grew here. This region is now the corn belt of America, and little of the original prairie is left.

To the east of the Rockies the land is generally higher, around 3,000 feet, and is much drier, being in the rain shadow of the mountains. On these semi-arid high plains, short grasses such as buffalo grass and blue gramma were abundant. The short height of these grasses makes them more resistant to drought than their eastern counterparts. This region is now used primarily for wheat farming, though it is not cultivated so intensively as the corn belt. Much of the area is still covered in the original vegetation, and cattle now graze where once the bison and pronghorn roamed. Outwardly, the scene is much the same as it was a hundred years ago. The region contains many plants often found in the semi-desert areas, such as the prickly pear cactus and the tumbleweed – a plant much loved by the directors of Hollywood Westerns!

A transition zone existed between the tall and short grass regions, where medium-sized grasses such as June grass, western wheat grass and little bluestem grew.

The prairie and grassland vegetation was not limited to grass, of course. A great variety of wild flowers were to be found in profusion. Despite the fact that much of the original landscape has been destroyed, some such areas can still be found, particularly in Oklahoma and Texas, which give an idea of what these grasslands were once like.

Members of the pea family and daisy family are particularly common in the prairies, but flowers from across the botanical spectrum: phloxes, prairie lilies, shooting stars, black-eyed susan, prairie roses and Texas bluebonnets, can be found. The last named is the state flower of Texas, which can turn entire fields a dazzling blue. Even where the original habitat has been lost, many of the flowers can still be found, often in large numbers, bordering fields and meadows. Most of these plants are perennials, their roots and stems forming mats which bind together the soft soils and protect them from the erosive powers of the rain.

Whilst the grasslands accounted for a third of the original vegetation cover of America, woodlands and forests occupied about half. Like the grasslands, they have been systematically destroyed – or irrevocably altered over the last hundred years. Large areas of woodland do still exist though, where many of America's most familiar and popular wild flowers are to be found. Woodland originally covered the entire eastern third of the country as well as occupying large areas of the West, while dense redwood forests grew along much of the Pacific coast.

The vast deciduous woodlands of the central region of the East were certainly the most luxuriant of the country, though none of the trees, large as they were, matched the height of the giant redwoods and sequoias of the West. They were very varied woodlands, consisting of red oak, which produces a spectacular display of color in the fall, hickory, chestnut, maple, tulip tree, redbud and flowering dogwood. The dogwood flowers in late spring, and has white or pink flower heads. Each head has four large petal-like bracts which look like single flowers, but in fact the actual flowers are very small and clustered in the center of these bracts.

Conifers are scattered throughout the region, with hemlock being common, particularly on the higher slopes. It was given its name by early foresters who thought that its foliage had a similar smell to European hemlock, an umbelliferous plant. Its timber has many uses, such as for wood pulp and packaging, whilst its bark is rich in tannin, used in the leather industry for curing hides. Other conifers of the region include shortleaf pine, pitch pine and scrub pine, while junipers are often found on drier, rocky slopes. The juniper is a very resilient plant which can withstand freezing winds, deep snow and summer drought. It usually grows as a low bush, and its leaves, which contain a pungent resin, have sharp tips, protecting the plant from grazing animals. Junipers bear purple berries in autumn, which are eaten by birds, who then disperse the seeds. These are generally too sour for human consumption, though they are used in the manufacture of gin.

This once vast, unbroken forest is now much reduced and fragmented as urban sprawl continues. In the areas that have survived, a great variety of wild flowers can be found. Many of these bloom in early spring, before the dense woodland canopy has fully developed and screened the sunlight from the forest floor. Many of these wild flowers are popular and familiar wild plants, as well as being some of the most beautiful. Among the first to appear are hepaticas, trout lilies, trilliums, violets and spring beauties, which signal an end to winter, often flowering while snow still lies on the ground.

The hepaticas are so called because of the resemblance of their leaves to the human liver. According to the *Doctrine of Signatures*, early herbalists believed that if a plant, or part of a plant, resembled a part of the human anatomy, it could be used to treat ailments of that part, so hepaticas have long been used for treating diseases of the liver! Many of America's wild plants have been used by native Indians and early settlers alike for treating a variety of conditions – plants such as boneset, lungwort, and the foul-smelling purple trillium, which was once used to treat gangrene.

The trilliums are members of the lily family. As the name implies, all parts of the flower and leaves are arranged in threes. There are many different species, and they are often called wake robins as they come into bloom at about the same time as the robin returns to the woodlands after journeying from its winter home in the South. Many of the trilliums have been used by native Indians for a variety of medicinal purposes as well as for food – the leaves were often cooked and eaten as greens. Many kinds of trillium are cultivated and grown in gardens.

Also blooming in the forests in these early months are many species of violet in a range of purples, yellows and white. They are generally small flowers, growing singly or in small clumps. A close inspection will show them to be simple, yet stunningly beautiful. They frequently hybridize, in many cases making precise identification difficult.

Other spring flowers include wild ginger, anemones, bloodroot, and two similar members of the poppy family: the beautiful Dutchman's breeches, and squirrel corn.

With the arrival of summer, the woodland interior becomes dark and shadowy as the leaf canopy develops. Few flowers are to be found in the heart of the wood now, perhaps just patches of Wild leek, white snakeroot and various goldenrods. Two plants well worth searching out at this time are the Indian pipe and its close relative the pinesap, more usually found in coniferous woods. These are saprophytic plants, lacking the chlorophyl necessary for them to carry out the process of photosynthesis. The Indian pipe is white and looks just as though someone had planted a clay pipe! Being saprophytic the plant gets its nutrients from the rich woodland humus in which it grows, enlisting the aid of a fungus to help it do so. This fungus forms a close "mycorrhizal" association with the roots. The plant may be from two to twelve inches tall, and often grows in large clumps. The flowers hang down to one side of the stem – the generic name *Monotropa* means turned to one side. The whole plant turns dark brown or black when the fruit is ripe. It has long been used by native Indians for the treatment of nervous disorders and sore eyes.

It is, of course, this great deciduous forest of the north-east which, in the fall, produces one of the world's most spectacular plant displays, as the oaks, maples and other trees change into a multitude of colors before shedding their leaves. The Appalachian region particularly is stunning, and a visit is an essential part of botanizing in America.

Moving southwards through the eastern part of the country, the more northerly species are replaced by trees such as longleaf pine, slash pine, magnolias, gums, pecans and persimmon. In the forests of the south, a higher proportion of the trees and shrubs are evergreen; not only the conifers, but also the broad-leaved trees such as sweet bay, live oak and southern magnolia. These have tough, leathery leaves, dark green on top and lighter underneath, which are well adapted to retain moisture in a climate which may include occasional winter frosts, spring drought and intense summer heat.

The woodlands of the south are quite varied, with those on the upland regions being a typical mixture of deciduous trees and just a few conifers, whilst on sandy soils the woodlands become dominated by pines, with an undergrowth of wire grass and saw palmetto. Saw palmetto is a dwarf palm with fan-shaped leaves and sharp spines on the leaf stalks. Large areas of swamp exist, particularly in southern Florida, where cypress trees, tupelos and sweet gums are common. In some areas, tropical hardwood trees with strange names such as bustic, mastic, gumbo-limbo and poisonwood are found.

The sub-tropical swamps and bayous of southern Florida, Georgia and Louisiana contain a number of fascinating plants not found elsewhere in America. Many species of epiphytes or "air-plant" are found, such as Spanish moss, which often festoons swamp cypresses with its long, trailing, tattered leaves. It is a bromeliad and member of the pineapple family. These epiphytes usually live on the branches and trunks of trees (and sometimes on telegraph poles!) and obtain most of their nutrients from minerals leached from the foliage of their host. They are not parasitic and can carry out photosynthesis. The Spanish moss is used by the swallow-tailed kite in the construction of its beautiful nest. There is even one species of epiphytic cactus, the mistletoe cactus, which has taken to a life in the air.

There are many other species of bromeliad in southern Florida, some of which hold rainwater in vase-like reservoirs at their base. Mosquitoes and tree-frogs breed in these, and many other animals drink from them in dry weather.

One particular tree starts its life as an epiphytic seedling on the branches of other trees, growing slowly, and eventually sending down long aerial roots to the ground, or entwining them around the host tree. This is eventually strangled and dies, leaving a large strangler fig in its place.

Another very large group of plants, which includes many epiphytic species, is the orchid family. To both the botanist and the layman, orchids hold a special place, often having stunning flowers, while being difficult to find. It often comes as a surprise to many people that orchids are to be found outside of the steamy tropical jungles with which they are normally associated. They are, in fact, found in all major habitats of the world, from the equator to the Arctic Circle, and in America they can be found growing above the timberline in the mountains, in forests, bogs and the grasslands.

Most of the orchids found in the forests of the southeast are epiphytes, having evolved specialized roots for clinging onto tree bark. The network of roots that forms entangles dead leaves and other plant debris, providing a reservoir of humus in which the absorbing roots grow. In common with most orchids, the epiphytes have minute, dust-like seeds which travel great distances on air currents.

Most of the American epiphytic orchids growing in the Florida Everglades grow in the dimly-lit interior of the tropical hardwood hammocks, though a few are found out in the open, growing on mangrove, willow and cocoplum. The butterfly and cowhorn orchids are both such sun-lovers, and both have a reservoir of rainwater at the base of their clustered leaves. The cowhorn is the largest of the orchids growing in these woods; some specimens have weighed up to seventy-five pounds. Unfortunately, many of these orchids have been over-collected, and are now very rare.

One of the most beautiful of epiphytic orchids is the night-blooming epidendrum. It flowers throughout the year, producing small, white blooms only two inches across, which are especially fragrant at night.

In the deciduous and coniferous forests further north, many of the orchids found there are saprophytes, lacking the green pigment chlorophyl. They are generally yellow or pink, and have branched, fleshy rhizomes which absorb nutrients from the decaying leaf litter in which they grow. Such plants are called coral root orchids, from the bizarre shape of the root mass. All orchids start their lives as saprophytes, depending on a fungus which grows in association with their roots. As their seeds are so tiny (to enable wind dispersal) they have no food reserve with which to begin their development. The seed is thus dependent on the presence of the fungus for its germination and subsequent development. The relationship continues throughout the life of the plant. Most orchids are very slow growing, and may take ten years or more from germination of the seed to flowering.

Many of the orchids have beautiful flowers, perhaps none more so than the lady's slipper orchids, where the lip of the flower forms a pouch into which insects are attracted. Once inside the flower, there is only one exit, past the stigma, where pollen from a previously-visited flower is brushed off. The insect must now go underneath the anthers, where new pollen is deposited onto its body. Many orchids have very specific relationships with their insect pollinators, having evolved specific features so that only the correct insect can pollinate the flower.

Many of America's orchids have been picked or dug up by collectors or growers to such an extent that they are endangered in the wild, only to be found now in nature reserves. Others are still relatively common, but could well become much scarcer if picking continues. Most of America's orchids do not thrive under cultivation, having very specific requirements, and should be left in their natural habitat for all to enjoy.

Along most of the west coast of America, and up into Canada and southern Alaska grow large areas of primarily coniferous woodland. In the northwest in particular, these form perhaps the world's best example of temperate rainforest. The winds here are predominantly southwesterly, blowing off the relatively warm Pacific. As they rise over the mountain ranges they are cooled, depositing large amounts of rain on the coastal belt. Temperatures are warm and humidity is high, leading to frequent mist and fog in many areas. This climate has encouraged the development of verdant evergreen forests, where some of the world's tallest and largest trees, the giant redwoods, grow. With their thick, soft, fibrous bark these are stout trees yielding strong, durable timber used by the lumber industry of the region. Their foliage closely resembles that of yew. Only tiny flowers are produced, both sexes on the same tree, which ripen into small cones containing the winged seeds. The largest specimens are today found preserved in national parks. Whilst they are not the largest or oldest trees, they do grow to an immense size, often over 300 feet tall, and over sixty feet in circumference. (Coast, or Californian redwoods have taller specimens, one measured at 370 feet in California, whilst the giant sequoias, or mammoth trees, are the world's stoutest, often measuring up to seventy feet in circumference.)

In the depths of these lush forests, mosses and ferns abound in the humid conditions, but flowers are scarce. Many that are found here are saprophytes, such as pinesap, candystick and striped coral root orchid. These absorb their nutrients from the rich, thick leaf litter, usually with the aid of a mycorrhizal fungus. Other flowers to be found in spring include the queen cup and large white trillium. The vanilla leaf, or deer foot is quite common, though mostly outside the redwood forests. It has small, white flowers and an unusual, deeply-cleft leaf which resembles the shape of a deer's foot. When dried, the leaves have a sweet smell, earning it its other name of sweet after death.

To many people, the most attractive flower of the Pacific coast woods is the Pacific dogwood, which often grows large enough to form an understory tree, particularly along the banks of forest streams. The conspicuous white bracts surrounding the tiny flowers seem to glitter in the dappled light of the forest. It is one of the few western trees whose foliage turns red in the fall. Other flowering shrubs include the Oregon grape, manzanita, madrona and blueblossom.

Natural clearings and glades provide the best opportunity for flowers to flourish. Here mariposa tulips or lilies can be very common, growing with lupines, foxgloves, columbines, bitterroot, balsam root, paintbrushes and salal. Wild clematis climbs over the trees, the blue flowers standing out well against the dark green foliage. The feathery seeds look very attractive in autumn. Looking like puffs of smoke when seen at a distance, bear grass has delicate white flower heads on the top of stout stalks, which may grow to a height of five feet from a large bunch of basal leaves. The plant is actually a lily. Indians used the leaves for weaving baskets and cloth, as well as eating the roasted rootstock.

In the more southerly areas of the Pacific coast the climate becomes drier and trees become smaller and sparser, intermingling eventually with the desert vegetation discussed earlier. One tree of note in the region is the bristlecone pine, one of the world's longest-living trees. It never attains a great size, but may persist, growing interminably slowly, for up to 5,000 years.

The last major habitat types in which wild flowers are found are the rivers and streams, ponds and lakes, marshes, bogs and swamps – the wetlands. Large areas of wetland are found across America, from the many streams flowing off the western mountains into the Pacific and the numerous lakes and bogs in the northern regions affected by glaciation, to the swamps and bayous of the south.

Out on the open water of lakes and quiet waters, perhaps the most familiar and characteristic flowers are the water lilies. The striking yellow pond, or bullhead lily is common, whilst the fragrant water lily has large white or pink flowers which open in the morning and close in the early afternoon. Large areas of water may be covered by the lily leaves, which die back at the end of each summer, contributing to the organic debris on the bottom of the lake.

Another aquatic is the pickerelweed, well known to fisherman seeking the pickerel fish, as fish and plant seem to occupy the same habitat. The interior of the leafstalk has large, loosely-packed cells, with sizeable air spaces between them. This allows oxygen to reach submerged parts of the plant, and gives maximum support with the minimum of tissue. The seeds can be eaten like nuts and the young leaves cooked and eaten as greens. They are also eaten by deer.

On the banks of lakes two species of lobelia are to be found: the vivid red cardinal flower, and the great blue lobelia. The cardinal flower is unusual in that most lobelias are blue or violet. It is pollinated mainly by hummingbirds, which can extract the nectar from its the long tubular base. The color of the flower is very similar to that of robes worn by Roman Catholic cardinals, hence the common name.

The blue flag, or wild iris, is another familiar plant of the water's edge, as well as being found in marshes and bogs, mainly in the north and east. It can grow in large stands, adding a splash of vivid blue color to the landscape from May to August. Its rhizome, or underwater stem, is reputed to be extremely poisonous.

In the marshy ground around a lake, several distinctive flowers grow. One of the most striking is the wild calla, or water arum, whose eye-catching white, hood-like spathes surround a vertical spadix covered in tiny yellow flowers. It bears red berries in the fall, as does its close relative, the jack-in-the-pulpit, a plant more usually found in damp woods. The red berries of the arums are no match for the winterberry, though. This is a deciduous holly shrub which bears copious amounts of berries – a spectacular sight.

Two other arums are found early in the year in the marshes and swamps. The skunk cabbage is one of the first flowers to appear in spring, sending up a brownish-purple mottled spathe surrounding a small spadix covered in tiny flowers. The heat arising from cellular respiration may actually melt snow or ice around the plant. As its name

would suggest, it has a strong, fetid smell which attracts insects. The yellow skunk cabbage is found more in the West, and may cover large areas with its brilliant yellow hoods, which can grow to a height of twenty inches.

Of all the wetland habitats it is the bog which is potentially the most interesting, yet least explored. Bogs are not static communities; they may be fully grown over or have open water at their center, though most will grow over in time. They are highly acidic and nearly always have sphagnum moss as their dominant plant. This may be present in clumps or spread out across the surface of the bog in knee-deep carpets. It is highly absorbent, holding many times its own weight of water.

Bogs have their own distinctive communities of plants either growing on the sphagnum, or on the wet, peaty ground. Plants such as buckbean, bog rosemary, leatherleaf, Labrador tea and the much cultivated cranberry are typical. In June and July several orchids can be found, including the swamp pink (sometimes called the dragon's mouth), the bog rein orchid, the rose pogonia, and two beautiful orchids: the golden yellow and the queen's lady's slippers. Blooming later than most other flowers is the lovely, sky-blue fringed gentian.

There is one group of plants growing here which never fails to attract the attention of botanists – the insectivorous plants. There are several families, the sundews, pitcher plants and butterworts are found on the surface of the bog, whilst the bladderwort is an aquatic plant, growing in open water. Another plant is the famous Venus fly trap, now found in only a small area around the town of Wilmington, in North Carolina.

All the insectivorous plants ensnare insects and invertebrates using a variety of traps. They then secrete enzymes which break down the body of the insect, providing the plant with a valuable source of nutrients not found in the poor soils of the bog.

The pitcher plant attracts insects by the colorful opening to the pitcher and by the nectar secreted by it. The inside of the pitcher is slippery and has numerous downward-pointing hairs to which the unfortunate insect cannot grip. It falls down into the pitcher where, in most species, rainwater has collected. The insect is drowned and subsequently digested by enzymes secreted by the plant.

Sundews are generally much smaller, and trap their prey on the sticky, glandular hairs of their leaves. Longer hairs at the edge of the leaf slowly fold down over the insect, putting it into contact with the digestive portion of the leaf. A carpet of sundews seems to glisten with dew when the sun shines on it. The flowers are generally small and inconspicuous.

Butterworts are similar, in that they trap insects on their leaves – in this case, sticky, fleshy leaves, whose sides curl inwards over the insect.

The aquatic bladderworts are fascinating in that their underwater roots have specialized bladders, which are elaborate traps. When small aquatic organisms, such as water fleas and mosquito larvae, brush against hairs near the opening, a tiny door springs open inwards, creating a rush of water that carries the insect with it. Comparatively large organisms can be trapped, being digested little by little. The bladderworts have yellow flowers which bloom on the top of stalks up to eight inches above the water surface.

Probably the most fascinating of the insectivores is the Venus fly trap, which traps its prey on remarkable leaves shaped very much like a mantrap. They are formed by a pair of rounded lobes hinged in the middle like a book, each with a line of long spikes along their outer edge. They lie almost flat on the ground and attract insects with their orange-red interior which secretes nectar. On the inside of each lobe are three "trigger-hairs." Insects such as flies land on the leaves. If only one hair is touched nothing happens (it might be a raindrop, for example), but if one is touched twice, or two or three are touched, then the two lobes spring shut, trapping the insect inside. The bristles around the edge interlock,

helping to keep the insect inside whilst the trap is shutting. The lobes then secrete digestive enzymes, and the body of the insect is broken down. The Venus fly trap has been intensively collected over the years, both by collectors and by commercial growers. It is now recognized as an endangered species and protected by law in North Carolina.

As we have seen, America has a tremendous range and diversity of wild flowers. Their distribution is the result of millions of years of evolution, and most species have been growing in the same place for thousands, if not millions, of years. Before the arrival of the European settlers, the native Indians lived in harmony with their environment, never wilfully destroying habitats or their plants. However, over the last two hundred years or so, vast areas have been destroyed, mostly for agricultural use, and with them their wild flowers. The settlers also brought plants, such as purple loosestrife, which, having no natural competition, have overrun many habitats, ousting the native plants. As if these pressures aren't enough, many plants have been brought to the verge of extinction by collectors, who can often obtain high prices for their specimens. Even the giant saguaros are not immune – good specimens can fetch up to $4,000 on the black market!

Yet there is a growing conservation movement in America: politicians now talk of conservation policies, and institutions such as the Wild Flower Research Center have been established recently to help preserve the wonderful heritage of America's wild flowers for future generations to enjoy.

Coastal Wildflowers

The coast, with its cliffs, sand dunes and shingle beaches, is a hostile environment for plants. The air is laden with salt and, even if they are not actually splashed with sea water, plants can be affected by sea spray for many miles inland. The wind blows constantly, so many coastal plants have developed long roots and flexible stems to resist its force. Whilst many coastal plants show specific adaptations to their particular environment, many are found in other habitats as well. In some areas, for example, mountain plants, such as mountain avens, moss campion and certain saxifrages, are found on seacliffs as well as in their more usual mountain habitats. One of the main problems for plants growing on the coast is desiccation by the wind, and many species develop a thick cuticle, or outer skin, over their leaves. Many also have hairs on their leaves to help reduce evaporation, whilst others grow in dense rosettes to conserve water. Some plants, such as glasswort, have succulent stems owing to water-retentive tissues. Succulence, in fact, is a common feature of plants in dry habitats. On constantly shifting sand dunes many plants have long roots and creeping stems which effectively stabilize the sand, preventing erosion. Sea bindweed, or beach morning glory, is one of these. Sand dunes tend to be rich in calcium, and many limestone-loving plants, including several orchids, are found on coastal sand dunes as well as in their normal limestone, grassland or woodland habitats.

Above: part of the Oregon coast, one of the various habitats in which coastal flowers can be found. Left: sea morning glory (*Ipomoea pes-caprae*), also known as the railroad vine. This showy plant was introduced from the West Indies. It grows on sand dunes and beaches, often right up to the water's edge. The specific name, meaning "goat's foot," refers to the shape of its leaves. Sea oats (*Uniola paniculata*) (right) is a grass which is often planted to stabilize sand dunes, protecting them from erosion.

Above: goldenrod (*Solidago sp.*) growing on sand at Cape May, New Jersey. It is one of the few plants that can grow in the rather unstable bare sand. Those that do usually have long, extensive, penetrating roots. There are numerous species of goldenrod throughout America, many of which are hard to identify. Facing page: sea morning glory (*Ipomoea pes-caprae*). This beautiful flower is often cultivated in gardens. It is a member of the same family of plants as convolvulus, a troublesome and noxious weed. The flower opens early in the morning and is closed by midday.

Above: slender glasswort (*Salicornia europaea*). Typical of coastal salt marshes, this succulent annual plant turns a spectacular red color in the fall. It colonizes bare mud where conditions are reasonably stable. It is found locally around the Great Lakes and the northern part of the east coast. It is edible, though very salty, and is used as a salad vegetable, raw or boiled. The name "glasswort" comes from the fact that it was once burnt to obtain soda ash, used for glass making. Minute, yellow flowers are produced between August and October in the axils of their fleshy stems. Silverweed (*Potentilla anserina*) (left) is a widespread member of the rose family, found primarily on sandy shores and in wet meadows. The basal leaves have a mass of silvery hairs on their underside, hence the common name. Its roots are edible, tasting rather like parsnips when boiled. Facing page: rugosa, or wrinkled rose (*Rosa rugosa*). This large rose was introduced from the Orient and is now found on the beaches and dunes of the Northeast westwards to Wisconsin and Illinois. It is often planted to help stabilize sand dunes, and it flowers from June to September.

Thrift (*Armeria maritima*) (top) is a widespread plant, found all round the coast of America. It flowers from March to July, and may cover large areas of clifftop with its posies of lilac-purple flowers. It is also found in mountainous and prairie regions. Roseroot (*Sedum rosea*) (above and facing page) is a succulent plant growing on eastern, rocky coastal cliffs as well as in mountainous regions, both in the east and west. The name sedum comes from the Latin verb "to sit," referring to the way in which many sedums grow close to the ground.

Below: beach verbena (*Abronia villosa*) at Monterey Bay, California. This attractive plant grows all over the Southwest, in desert regions as well as on sandy beaches along the coast. It blooms from March up until October. The flower stems can reach ten inches in height, but the trailing ground stems may extend for as much as three

feet. Beach morning glory (*Calystegia soldanella*) (facing page) is common on sandy or shingle beaches. Blooming from April to September, the flowers open in the morning and stay open later into the afternoon than other morning glories. It is also a good stabilizer of sand dunes and its flowers are a favored source of food for rabbits.

Marsh and Wetland Wildflowers

Wetlands are special places for plants. The various wetland habitats, such as bogs, swamps, marshes, lakes, ponds and streams, all have their own characteristic range of species. Some plants grow on the permanently wet surface of bogs, whilst others are adapted to a totally aquatic life, growing largely immersed in the water, usually with part of them floating on the water surface. Perhaps the most familiar of the floating plants are the various water lilies, which can carpet large areas of water with their dense foliage. Along the margins of lakes, large colonies of cattails may grow, along with several species of lobelia, including the great blue lobelia and the striking scarlet cardinal flower, which attracts hummingbirds to its blooms. Blue flags are also common in this environment, as is the vigorous invader from Europe, the purple loosestrife. Swamps are home to a number of interesting plants, including three members of the arum family: the skunk cabbage, the yellow, or western, skunk cabbage, and the wild calla, or bog arum, all unmistakable! Bogs, however, are relatively unexplored, and contain some fascinating plants, including insectivorous plants, which ensnare insects and small invertebrates by a variety of devices. The creature, being caught, is then digested by processes through which the plant gains valuable nutrients. These plants include sundews, pitcher plants, the famous Venus' flytrap and the totally aquatic bladderwort.

Above: the delicate wild iris, or blue flag, (*Iris versicolor*) blooming in July in a typical Michigan woodland swamp. This beautiful iris is found in many northeastern woods and wetlands. Left: western skunk cabbage (*Lysichitum americanum*) growing along a woodland stream in May. The pungent, skunk-like odor from the sap and the fetid odor of the flowers attracts flies as pollinators. The sap was once used as treatment for ringworm. Right: water hyacinth (*Eichhornia crassipes*). This plant was introduced from the tropics and is now choking many southern waterways and shading out many of the native aquatic plants. Millions of dollars are spent each year to control it, particularly in Florida's Everglades. Overleaf: cattails (*Typha latifolia*) in a woodland swamp in Michigan.

Wild calla, or bog arum, (*Calla palustris*) (these pages), also known as the water arum, is the most northerly of the arums found in America and grows in cool swamps and bogs across the northern states of America and into Canada. Growing in water and flowering from May to August, it is often planted for ornamental purposes. The flowers are minute and clustered around a one-and-a-half-inch-long spadix, surrounded by a striking white, hood-like spathe. In the fall it produces a cluster of bright red berries.

The striking flowers of the buckbean, or bogbean, (*Menyanthes trifoliata*) (facing page and below) are found in bogs and ponds throughout much of America between May and August. Their flower stalks often reach a height of twelve inches above the water's surface and the buds are rose-pink, developing into boa-like, fringed white flowers. Buckbeans have two types of flower – those with long stamens and a short style, and those with short stamens and a long style. This ensures that cross-pollination takes place by the insect pollinators. Right: greater bladderwort (*Utricularia vulgaris*). The bladderworts are aquatic, insectivorous plants. They have small bladders on their underwater stems with a trapdoor-like flap at one end. Trigger hairs surround this door and if small creatures, such as water fleas or mosquito larvae, touch these, the door swings open very rapidly, causing water and the creature to be swept into the bladder. This stimulates the plant to produce enzymes which dissolve the prey. Nutrients are released by this process which are then absorbed by the plant. The yellow flowers appear between May and September on stalks protruding from one to four inches above the water's surface. This plant is found throughout much of North America, usually in lakes and ponds with acidic, still waters.

Pitcher plants (*Sarracenia purpurea*) (these pages) are another type of insectivorous plant and grow in nutrient-poor, acidic peat bogs, usually amongst sphagnum moss. The vase-shaped pitcher has slippery, downward-pointing hairs. Insects are attracted to the pitcher by a combination of its scent and color. When they land on the plant they cannot grip onto the hairs and fall into the water-filled pitcher where they drown. Enzymes are secreted by the plant which break down the insect's body, releasing nutrients which are then absorbed by the plant. Its striking flower (facing page) blooms between May and August on stalks often as tall as two feet.

The skunk cabbage (*Symplocarpus foetidus*) (above and facing page) is one of the earliest flowers to appear in spring, often when snow is still lying on the ground. Heat from the plant's cellular respiration actually melts the snow or ice around it. It is a member of the arum family and produces minute, creamy flowers on a two- to six-inch-high spadix. This is surrounded by a modified leaf, known as a spathe, which has a distinctive mottled, purplish appearance. Later in the year, large cabbage-like leaves appear, which may be dense enough to apparently carpet an area. The fetid scent, produced especially when the plant is bruised, is reminiscent of skunk spray – which explains the plant's name. Pollinating insects are attracted to the flowers by their scent. Skunk cabbage is found in many northeastern swamps, marshes and wet woodlands, extending as far south as Georgia, and west to Iowa. Left: the western, or yellow, skunk cabbage (*Lysichitum americanum*) is another arum; in this case its spathes have a distinctive bright yellow color. Like its eastern relative, it flowers early in the year, often before the snow has melted. It too has an offensive odor which draws flies to pollinate it. It is a favorite springtime food of bears, which eat both the leaves and the fleshy underground stem. The stem was also used by native Indians, who baked it to supplement their winter diet.

Marsh marigold, or cowslip, (*Caltha palustris*) (above) flowers early, growing in swamps, wet meadows and along stream banks throughout much of northern America. Its brilliant yellow flowers have no petals – instead they have from five to nine petal-like sepals. Fragrant white water lily (*Nymphaea*

odorata) (facing page) blooms from June to September, opening its flowers in the early morning and closing them by midday. It is found on most stretches of quiet water throughout eastern America. Overleaf: yellow water lily (*Nuphar polysepala*).

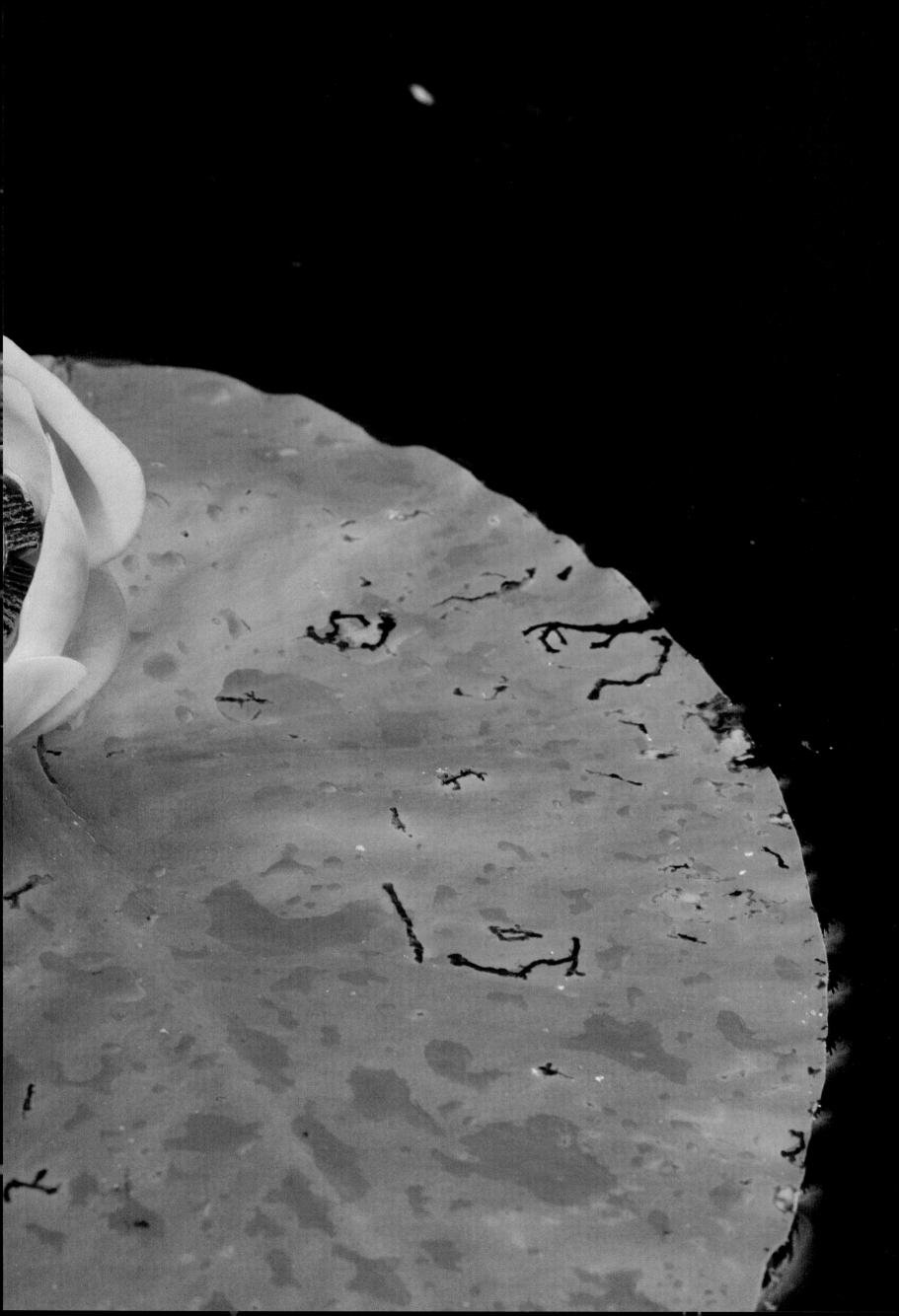

These pages: leafless ghost orchids (*Polyrrhiza lindenii*) in the Florida Everglades. These are some of the many "air-plants," or epiphytes, found in southern Florida. They live non-parasitically on trees – their roots, whilst absorbing some nutrients,act primarily as anchors. They produce minute, dust-like seeds and it is thought that, over the centuries, most of Florida's orchids arrived on the wind from South America and the West Indies.

These pages: yellow lady's slipper orchids (*Cypripedium calceolus*). These charming wildflowers have become scarce in recent years due to extensive picking by collectors. They grow, both in woodlands and swamps, to a height of about thirty inches. Their common name refers to the distinctive yellow pouch formed by the lowest petal. The top and side petals vary in color from yellow to purple. Overleaf: pink lady's slipper orchids (*Cypripedium acaule*) growing amid sphagnum moss in wet woodland in Michigan.

The elephant heads plant (*Pedicularis groenlandica*) (facing page) is found over wet meadows, along cold streams throughout the western mountains, across the Boreal forests of North America and in many places along the Atlantic coast. The flower's shape resembles a miniature elephant's head, its lowest petal forming the trunk. This flower pattern evolved to facilitate pollination – pollen is placed by the flower in a precise position on any visiting insect so that when it visits another flower pollen is efficiently transferred. The flowers bloom from June to August, each spike reaching a height of about thirty inches. Above: a great blue lobelia (*Lobelia siphilitica*) covered in dew. This beautiful blue flower is fairly common in swamps, wet meadows and woods, mainly in the northeast of the United States. It is often cultivated in gardens, and its specific name comes from its supposed ability to cure syphilis. The roots contain strong alkaloid chemicals which induce vomiting.

These pages: California corn lily (*Veratrum californicum*). This highly poisonous plant is found in the Southwest, in California, Colorado, Wyoming, Montana and into New Mexico. It grows in swamps and creeks, as well as in wet meadows and damp woodland. Animals eating the plant often produce deformed young, and honeybees and other insects may even die after foraging on the flowers, which bloom from June to August and may grow up to eight feet tall.

These pages: wild iris, or blue flag (*Iris versicolor*). This plant, common in the Northeast, is found along rivers as well as in marshes and other wet habitats. Its underwater rhizome, though extremely poisonous, was dried by Indians and used medicinally. The flowers are pollinated by insects which are attracted to the sepals. To reach them they have to crawl under the style and brush past a stigma and stamen, thus pollinating the flower.

These pages: purple loosestrife (*Lythrum salicaria*). This very attractive flower makes a spectacular show, covering large areas of wetland. It is, however, a species introduced from Europe and is very strong-growing, shading out many of the indigenous wetland plants which are of more value to native wildlife.

These pages: the cardinal flower (*Lobelia cardinalis*), unusual in that most lobelias are blue or violet in color. This particularly brilliant lobelia attracts hummingbirds, which extract the nectar from its elongated, tubular base with their long tongues. It grows to a height of six feet in wetland habitats over much of the country, blooming from July to September. The scarlet color is similar to that of robes worn by Roman Catholic cardinals, hence the name.

The Venus' flytrap (*Dionaea muscipula*) (left) is the most famous of the insectivorous plants of America, growing only within a fifty-mile radius of the town of Wilmington in North Carolina, where it is strictly protected. The traps at the end of its leaf blades have six trigger hairs. If an insect, such as a wasp, or other small invertebrate, touches only two of these, the two halves of the trap snap shut, catching the insect inside. This stimulates the secretion of an enzyme which breaks down the body of the insect, releasing nutrients in the process. These are then absorbed by the plant and the trap is reset. Small white flowers are produced in May and June on four- to twelve-inch-high stalks. Below, facing page and overleaf: round-leaved sundew (*Drosera rotundifolia*). The sundews are another type of insectivorous plant, found mainly in nutrient-poor bogs. Insects, such as damselflies (overleaf), crawling over or flying into the sticky leaves become trapped and are slowly digested by enzymes secreted by the plant.

Fringed gentians – (*Gentiana detonsa*) (above), and (*Gentiana crinita*) (facing page) – with their gorgeous blue color and fringed petals, are among the loveliest of America's wildflowers. *Gentiana detonsa* blooms in the western mountains, whilst *Gentiana crinita* is a more eastern species, flowering in late August and persisting until the winter frosts.

Woodland and Forest Wildflowers

Woodland flowers are some of America's most familiar and popular plants. A springtime walk in a deciduous wood, no matter how small, is a must for people who enjoy seeing the return of old favorites, such as hepatica, spring beauty, trilliums (or wake robins, as they are sometimes called), violets and trout lilies each year. These flowers bloom early in the year, before the forests' leafy canopy develops and blocks out much of the light from the woodland floor. A little later in the year several species of orchid can be found, such as the pink lady's slipper and the striped coralroot. This last plant is, like several other woodland flowers, a saprophyte, which means that, unable to manufacture its own food, it gains its nutrients from leaf litter. Unfortunately, many orchids have become rare in recent years due to overpicking. Coniferous forests are generally much darker and less congenial to plants than deciduous ones. Even so, a number of characteristic species are found, such as the lovely twinflower, wintergreens, pyrolas and another orchid, often found growing in large numbers, the calypso. Most woodlands are not merely uniform groups of trees; some have glades and clearings where more light penetrates, whilst others may have wet areas, where a totally different range of flowers will flourish. In the subtropical Florida Everglades, for example, hardwood trees grow on islands amid the mangrove swamps and are often festooned with epiphytic orchids, among others. The diversity of America's woodlands is matched by the diversity of the plants which they contain.

Above: white fringed phacelia (*Phacelia fimbriata*). This pretty flower is found in the upland woods of the east, from Virginia to Alabama, and is particularly abundant in the Great Smoky Mountains. It flowers in May and June. Pacific dogwood (*Cornus nuttallii*) (left) grows throughout the forests of the West, often reaching a height of sixty feet or more. It has superb red foliage in the fall. Right: wake-robin (*Trillium grandiflorum*). Many species of trillium grow in America's woodlands, generally coming into flower in early spring, at about the same time as the robin arrives from its migration – hence the common name. "Trillium" refers to the three-part structure of the plant: three petals, three sepals and three leaves.

Above: the unfurling leaves of devil's club (*Oplopanax horridum*). This large plant grows to a height of ten feet in the woodlands of the West. It has long, sharp spines, which can cause painful swelling. The small, whitish flowers are followed in the fall by handsome scarlet berries. The Indian pipe plant (*Monotropa uniflora*) (facing page) is a saprophytic plant growing on the leaf litter of woodland floors throughout the United States.

Dutchman's breeches (*Dicentra cucullaria*) (below) are some of the most distinctive flowers in America's woodlands. Appearing in April and May in many woodlands east of the Rockies, the uniquely shaped, fragrant flowers, resembling a pair of white pantaloons, are pollinated by those early bumblebees which have a proboscis long enough to reach the nectar. The plant grows up to a height of twelve inches. Facing page: fire pink contrasting with ferns (*Silene virginica*) in North Carolina. Its brilliant-red flowers appear from April to June in woods and thickets over much of eastern America, and are, in many cases, pollinated by hummingbirds. The plant is covered in sticky hairs which trap insects landing or crawling over it, although it does not feed on them. Another common name for this flower and others of the same genus is "catchfly."

Above and overleaf: calypso orchids (*Calypso bulbosa*). This exquisite orchid has become rather scarce over the last few years, though it does occasionally grow in very large colonies. It is found throughout much of the United States, usually in cool, damp, often coniferous woods, wherever there is a rich, thick litter. It flowers in May and June and reaches a maximum height of just eight inches. Left: pink lady's slipper orchid (*Cypripedium acaule*). One of several types of lady's slipper orchid in America, this bloom is so called because of the slipper-like shape of its bottom petal – indeed, another common name for this plant is the "moccasin flower." It blooms from April to July, mainly in dry, coniferous forests throughout much of America. Like the calypso, it often grows in large colonies, where several hundred at a time flower in a small area. The purple fringed orchid (*Habenaria fimbriata*) (facing page) has striking, heavily scented, fringed flowers. These are clustered around a leafy stem with large, eight-inch leaves at its base and smaller ones at the top. This grows to a height of four feet in the cool, damp woods of the East, and blooms from June to August. Moths are attracted to the flowers and extend their proboscises into the deep spur of the lip petal. As the proboscis is withdrawn, sticky pollen masses, also called pollinia, attach themselves to the moth's head. When the moth visits another flower the pollinia come off, thus ensuring that pollen is efficiently transferred from one flower to another.

Above: pink lady's slipper orchids (*Cypripedium acaule*) growing amid sphagnum moss. The showy lady's slipper orchid (*Cypripedium reginae*) (facing page) is the tallest and, arguably, the most attractive of all American orchids. Growing throughout much of the East, mainly on the limestone soils of moist woods and swamps, it has, unfortunately, been overpicked by collectors and has become very scarce in some areas. The glandular hairs on its leaves can cause a rash similar to that produced by poison ivy.

Above: bloodroot (*Sanguinaria canadensis*). This is a member of the poppy family and, like other poppies, its flowers last for a relatively short time. They open in full sun and close up at night. The flower stalk grows alongside a single basal leaf which often curls around the stalk. It is found in rich woods throughout much of North America, blooming from March to May. The plant was much used by Indians because, when cut open, its underground stem exudes a red sap, ideal as a dye and as war paint. This sap was also used to cure a variety of disorders, from coughs and colds to various skin diseases, as well as being used as an insect repellent. Left: Canada violets (*Viola canadensis*) in Michigan. These are common to northern woods and some mountain regions in spring. Their white flowers are slightly fragrant and appear from April onwards. Many species of violet grow all across America, in a wide range of colors – from white and yellow to blue and purple – and many are difficult to identify precisely. Facing page: large-flowered trillium (*Trillium grandiflorum*) and violets (*Viola sp.*) growing together in North Carolina woodland – a familiar springtime scene in most woodlands of the east. Trilliums, or wake-robins, are popular wildflowers and are often cultivated in gardens. They are members of the lily family. The leaves can be cooked and eaten as a green vegetable, though this may kill the plant as the rootstock can die if the leaves are not present to replenish the stored nutrients each year.

These pages: jack-in-the-pulpit (*Arisaema triphyllum*). This
distinctive member of the arum family grows in damp woods
and swamps throughout much of the East. In spring the
flower-bearing spadix appears inside a large, streaked spathe
and, in the fall, a cluster of bright red berries forms on the
spadix.

Above: clam shell orchid (*Epidendrum cochleatum*) in the Florida Everglades, where it grows as an epiphyte in the dimly lit, tropical hardwood hammocks and cypress sloughs. Facing page: dogtooth violet (*Erythronium grandiflorum*). This is, in fact, a lily, found in the west of the country, where it can carpet acres of ground – often as soon as the snow recedes. Also known as the "yellow fawn lily," it grows to a height of twelve inches.

Striped coral root orchid (*Corallorhiza striata*) (facing page) is a saprophytic orchid, unable to manufacture its own food by photosynthesis. Instead it relies on nutrients which it obtains from the rich leaf litter of the woodland floor where it grows. It is widespread throughout American woodlands, appearing in May, and its name refers to the tangled mass of root-like stems beneath the ground's surface. Above: western wood lily (*Lilium philadelphicum*). This lovely flower is found in meadows and forests throughout the western mountains, as well as on the adjoining prairies. It blooms in early summer from a bulb once used as a food by Indians, who cooked it in the same way as a potato.

Hepatica (*Hepatica americana*) (left), with its beautiful lavender-blue flowers, is one of the earliest woodland plants to appear in spring. It is generally found in dry, rocky woods, growing to a height of just six inches. The leaf is supposed to resemble the human liver and, according to the *Doctrine of Signatures*, was used by early herbalists for treating disorders of the liver, hence the name hepatica. Below: spring beauty (*Claytonia lanceolata*), and (facing page) Carolina spring beauty (*Claytonia caroliniana*). As the name implies, these flowers are also to be found early in the year. They grow from underground tubers, which were used as food by Indians and early colonists. They often grow in large patches, and make a spectacular show in early spring. *Claytonia caroliniana* is found primarily in the damp woods of eastern mountains, whilst *Claytonia lanceolata* is usually found in the western mountains. Overleaf: fringed polygala, or gaywings, (*Polygala paucifolia*) amid sphagnum moss in Michigan. This is a member of the milkwort family, once given to nursing mothers to improve milk flow. Generally a small plant, usually growing to six inches high or so in rich, damp woods, its attractive flowers appear during May. These flowers are complex, having two outer sepals and three united petals, forming a tube. The lowest petal ends in a finely fringed yellow or pink crest.

Grassland and Prairie Wildflowers

North America's prairies and grasslands once stretched in an unbroken band, some 2,000 miles long and 800 miles wide, up along the eastern side of the Rocky Mountains, through Kansas and Oklahoma, Wyoming and Montana and on into Canada, extending as far as the edge of the great Boreal forest. They were the largest and richest of all the world's grasslands; the home of vast herds of bison which grazed the vegetation and fertilized the soil, and of other grazers, such as pronghorn. Early settlers soon discovered the excellent soils and good climate and set about converting the prairies into agricultural land. The herds of bison have now gone and the once flower-filled grasslands are fragmented, preserved in their natural state in only a few places. Even so, certain areas do still exist where wildflowers bloom in abundance and produce spectacular displays in spring and summer. However, it is now hard to distinguish between the three major zones of grassland – the short, medium and tallgrass – each with its own characteristic range of species. The tallgrass prairie, whilst supporting perhaps three dominant grasses, has up to eighty different species of grass throughout its range, much of which may grow up to six feet tall and more. In among the grasses is an incredible diversity of flowers of many plant families – lupins, daisies, sunflowers, poppies, lilies, locoweeds and many, many more can be found, often in great abundance. In some areas, drifts of owl's clover or Texas bluebonnets extend as far as the eye can see. In other places, the prairie will seem to be on fire as prairie smoke waves its feathery seed heads in the breeze, creating the impression of smoke drifting across the land. So, whilst much of the natural grassland has been destroyed, areas do still exist where flowers can be found in abundance, and these are well worth searching for.

Owl's clover (*Orthocarpus purpuracens*) (above) can carpet many acres of grassland in early spring with its beautiful purple flowers. Left: spring wildflowers in Texas: evening primroses (*Oenothera sp.*) and paintbrushes (*Castilleja sp.*). As their name implies, evening primroses open their flowers in the early evening to be pollinated by moths. There are many species of paintbrush, named after the Spanish botanist, Castillejo. Right: rough blazing star (*Liatris aspera*) flowers in tallgrass prairie. This plant attracts many butterflies, such as the monarch, and grows to a height of four feet. Some of the tall grasses grow eight or nine feet tall.

Owl's clover (*Orthocarpus purpuracens*) (above) is a member of the figwort family. It is known as *escobita* in Spanish, meaning "little broom," and blooms from March to May. Facing page: pink evening primrose (*Oenothera speciosa*), and (overleaf) Texas prairie in April, blooming with Texas bluebonnets (*Lupinus subcarnosus*) and phlox (*Phlox sp.*). The bluebonnet is the Texan state flower and produces a spectacular floral display in April and May.

Top: day lilies (*Hemerocallis fulva*). This plant is a native of Europe and does not produce fertile seed, but reproduces vegetatively from the roots. Its flowers last for just one day. Butterfly weed (*Asclepias tuberosa*) (above) attracts large numbers of butterflies to its bright orange flowers. Indians used to chew its tough root as a cure for lung disorders, such as pleurisy. California poppies (*Eschscholtzia californica*) (facing page and overleaf) are the state flower of California and can produce superb displays in the grasslands, beginning as early as February.

Facing page: adobe lily (*Fritillaria pluriflora*). This is one of many fritillaries growing in the mountains and grasslands of America. It grows only on the grassy hills of California's Coast Ranges northwards to Oregon and blooms from February to April. The adobe lily is rather rare and is considered to be an endangered species. Above: sunflower (*Helianthus sp.*) in the dewy early morning. Sunflowers are found throughout North America and several varieties are cultivated for their oily seeds.

Above: Texas prairie in spring, thick with Indian paintbrush (*Castilleja sp.*) (facing page) in bloom. The paintbrushes belong to a huge, largely western genus within the figwort or snapdragon families. Most are bright red or orange, just a few being yellow, and they can be very difficult to identify positively. Many are semiparasitic, attaching themselves to the roots of other plants and obtaining some of their nutrients this way. For this reason they cannot be transplanted to gardens, or grown from seed. The flowers are complex, their bright colors coming not from the petals but from the calyx and bracts. The rest of the flower is small and protrudes like a beak through the bracts – its whole appearance is that of having been dipped in a pot of paint! They can be found growing singly, in small clumps or massed in their thousands in fields to create a wonderful display. Indian blanket (*Gaillardia pulchella*) (left) is a member of the daisy family. It is very variable, being found in many colors as well as variations to the structure of the flower itself: for example, it can occasionally be found lacking the ray flowers. It flowers from June to July in prairies and grasslands as well as on roadsides and field margins.

The death camas (*Zigadenus elegans*) (facing page) is highly poisonous. It blooms from June to August over meadows, rocky slopes and forests, growing up to a height of thirty inches. Prairie smoke (*Geum triflorum*) (above) blooms from April onwards in dry fields and prairies. Three pink flowers grow on one stem and the whole plant is hairy. The seeds have a long, silky tail and, when growing in large numbers, the plants give the illusion of smoke floating across the prairies. Overleaf: prostrate bluets (*Houstonia sp.*) and a dandelion.

Bitterroot (*Lewisia rediviva*) (above) is the state flower of Montana and has given its name to the Bitterroot Range and Bitterroot River. It has pink flowers, varying in shade, which have between twelve and eighteen petals growing from a small rosette of narrow, succulent leaves. It is found only in the West in open areas among pines or sagebrush, blooming right through from March to July. The large rootstock is intensely bitter when raw, but was eaten by Indians and early colonists when cooked. An odd characteristic of the roots is their ability to regenerate, perhaps many months after being dried. One specimen in a herbarium was placed in the ground a year after uprooting and went on to produce flowers again. This ability gave rise to the specific name of *rediviva*. Left: common harebell (*Campanula rotundifolia*). These pretty flowers are found throughout the western mountains, blooming from June to September. Fireweed, or rosebay willowherb, (*Epilobium angustifolium*) (facing page) is a colonist of burnt ground and was among the first plants to be found on the lava slopes of Mount St. Helens after its recent eruption. Ohio spiderwort (*Tradescantia ohiensis*) (overleaf) is found throughout the Midwest. It is one of several spiderworts found mainly in woodland habitats throughout America. The genus is named after John Tradescant, a member of a famous plant-collecting family, who is credited with first growing the plants in England. Recent research has shown that spiderworts' reaction to radiation is a good indicator of human response to radiation exposure.

Bear grass (*Xerophyllum tenax*) (above) is, in fact, a lily. It grows in woodland clearings over much of the west, to a height of approximately five feet. The flower stalk grows from the center of a large bunch of long, narrow basal leaves, and flowers from May to August. The plant was used extensively by Indians, both for food, and weaving – the long, fibrous leaves were woven to produce clothes and baskets. Teasel (*Dipsacus sylvestris*) (left) was originally introduced from Europe where it was used extensively in the woollen industry for raising the nap on cloth. It now grows wild throughout much of the East, reaching a height of six feet or more. The flowers start to open in July in a band around the center of the spike. New ones open daily in both directions, forming two distinct bands of flowers. The upper leaves are joined at their base around the stem to form a "cup" in which water often collects. The seeds are a favorite of many birds in winter. Thorn apple, or jimsonweed, (*Datura stramonium*) was introduced from tropical America and is now found in fields, meadows and waste places throughout the country. This foul-smelling plant is also highly poisonous and can cause dermatitis if touched. Its flowers are white or violet and trumpet-shaped and appear from July through to October. The name "thorn apple" comes from its prickly fruit (facing page).

Black-eyed Susan (*Rudbeckia hirta*) (these pages) is a common flower of the prairies and grasslands and is commonly cultivated in gardens. It blooms from June to October, often in great profusion, and is the state flower of Maryland. Facing page: black-eyed Susan growing on prairie in Ohio, along with other typical grassland plants such as mullein, yarrow and phlox.

Alpine Wildflowers

Many of the plants found in the mountains of America, particularly the western ranges, are also found in the Arctic tundra regions of Alaska and, indeed, the two habitats can be very similar. Temperatures can drop very low and the ground be frozen for long periods. Therefore, the plant sap of many species is viscous and acts rather like antifreeze, preventing the tissues from freezing. Summers are short, so many of the flowers have to bloom and set seed quickly. They are often brightly colored to attract insect pollinators, and may track the sun to absorb as much heat as possible. Winds can be ferocious and almost constant. They have the effect of taking water away from the plants, so many species have evolved low-growing, cushion shapes which cut down wind resistance, reducing the wind's desiccating effect as well as retaining heat. Many alpine meadows become carpeted with flowers almost as soon as the snow has disappeared from them, but their splendor is short-lived as the brief summer gives way to winter once more.

Facing page: avalanche lilies (*Erythronium montanum*) and subalpine buttercups (*Ranunculus sp.*) in Olympic National Park, Washington. This lily often comes into bloom just after the snow melts, carpeting huge areas with its beautiful white flowers. A visit to an alpine flower meadow in spring is a "must" for anyone interested in flowers. James' saxifrage (*Telesonix jamesii*) (right) is found high in the western mountains. There are many saxifrages, often growing from thin rock crevices, giving the appearance of having split the rock. The name "saxifrage" means "rock-breaker". Below: alpine meadow in Olympic National Park, Washington.

Shooting star (*Dodecatheon pauciflorum*) (above) grows in damp meadows throughout the western mountains. There are about ten species of pink-flowered shooting stars growing here, many of which are difficult to identify positively. They are members of the primrose family and their petals are bent sharply backwards, whilst their stamens form the point of the dart-like flower. Blooming from May to August, shooting stars grow to a height of approximately two feet. Avalanche lilies (*Erythronium montanum*) (facing page) flourish across northern Oregon to British Columbia, in high alpine and subalpine meadows, and grow up to ten inches high.

Above: mountain avens (*Dryas octopetala*). This plant is found in rocky alpine and tundra regions across North America and is a member of the rose family. It is generally a small, prostrate plant, often growing in large patches. Its small leaves, the edges of which roll inwards, are covered with hairs on their lower surface. Several types of Arctic poppies (*Papaver sp.*) (left) grow in the alpine and Arctic-tundra regions of North America, and are quite difficult to identify. They are generally low-growing, perhaps to a height of just four or five inches, and come into flower soon after the snow has melted. Facing page: glacier lilies (*Erythronium grandiflorum*) in Montana. Also called yellow fawn lilies, these flowers can, like the avalanche lily, carpet large areas of ground as the snow recedes.

Mountain avens (*Dryas octopetala*) (facing page) is a low-growing alpine plant whose white, parabolic flowers track the sun to absorb as much heat as possible. Above: purple mountain saxifrage (*Saxifraga oppositifolia*) growing in the typical low cushion shape of many alpines. This form cuts down resistance to the fierce winds and retains heat well – it can be as much as 10°C warmer within the cushion than the surrounding air. It is found generally throughout the alpine regions of the northern hemisphere.

Top: alpine locoweed (*Oxytropis podocarpa*), and (above) mountain pride (*Penstemon newberryi*), one of many penstemons found throughout America. Penstemons grow in rocky places from southwest Oregon to south of the Sierra Nevada in California. Bearberry, or kinnikinnick,

(*Arctostaphylos uva-ursi*) (facing page) is a member of the heather family. It was used extensively by Indians both as a medicine and a tobacco substitute, to which the name kinnikinnick refers, and its berries are a favorite food of bears.

Grass widows (*Sisyrinchium inflatum*) (facing page) are one of several similar species of blue-eyed grass, all of which are members of the lily family. This species occasionally has white flowers. Mountain globemallow (*Iliamna rivularis*) (above) grows along stream banks and in boggy areas over the western mountains as far south as Utah and Colorado.

Above: alpine forget-me-not (*Eritrichium elongatum*). This is one of several similar forget-me-nots found in the western mountains, all of which are covered in dense, woolly hairs. Indeed, the genus name eritrichium comes from the Greek meaning "woolly hair." Like other alpines it tends to be low-growing, and forms a cushion-like posy of flowers. Its blue petals attract bees to pollinate the flowers. Another alpine forget-me-not, *Myosotis alpestris* (left), belongs to a different genus within the forget-me-not, or borage, family. The pasqueflower (*Anemone patens*) (facing page) is the state flower of South Dakota. It comes into bloom early in the year, often before the snow has completely melted, and frequently flowers through until August. The word *pasque* comes from the old French word for Easter. The flower is covered in a dense layer of fine hair and grows to a height of ten inches or so. Its flowers lack petals, having purple, blue, or occasionally white, sepals, and its seeds have long, feathery plumes which are easily blown away by the wind.

Pink mountain heather (*Phyllodoce empetriformis*) (these pages), often the dominant plant over wide areas, grows on open, rocky slopes or in forests high in the western mountains from Alaska down to northern California and into Idaho and Colorado. It has deep pink, bell-shaped flowers with short, thin leaves, and blooms from June to August, growing to a height of eighteen inches or so. Facing page: Mount Rainier National Park in Washington.

Lewis' monkey flower (*Mimulus lewisii*) (top and facing page) is arguably one of the most attractive of all the mountain flowers. It blooms between June and August, attracting hummingbirds to pollinate its deep pink to red flowers. It tends to grow in wet places, such as on the banks of streams.

Moss campion, or cushion pink, (*Silene acaulis*) (above) resembles the purple saxifrage, but is actually a pink, a totally different family. Like the saxifrage, it has a low, cushion-like form and grows in damp areas high in the mountains throughout the northern hemisphere.

DesertWildflowers

American desert landscapes are among the most spectacular in the world and contain some of the most interesting and remarkable plants. Such arid regions might, at first, be thought to support little in the way of wildlife but they are, in fact, home to a wonderful array of plants, from magnificent saguaro cacti and Joshua trees to the delicate cactus blooms and other flowers which can appear in profusion after sufficient rain. In areas where rainfall is scarce, plants either have the ability to store water in their tissues, or to flower and set seed quickly, taking advantage of the infrequent rains. Their seeds are usually long-lived, lying dormant in the soil for many years until the right conditions for germination occur.

Above: typical desert vegetation in Arizona, including saguaro cacti (*Cereus gigantea*) and cholla (*Opuntia sp.*), and (left) the Sonoran Desert in Arizona, with cholla (*Opuntia sp.*) and brittlebush, or incienso, (*Encelia farinosa*). Right: the Arizona desert flowering with California poppies (*Eschscholtzia californica*) after rainfall. Many flowers are capable of producing shoots within hours of a rain shower, in an effort to flower and set seed before the land becomes parched once again. The seeds of poppies can survive for many years in the dry soil, waiting for the right conditions in which to germinate. Large areas of land are often carpeted with these and other flowers within days of rain.

Above: Chinese houses (*Collinsia heterophylla*). This lovely wildflower is found throughout California and south into Baja California. The flowers grow in rings around the stem, resembling a Chinese pagoda. Facing page: prickly poppy (*Argemone platyceras*) in Arizona. This is one of several similar, highly toxic species. However, its spiny fruits and foliage deter livestock from eating it.

Desert sunflowers (*Gerea canescens*) (facing page top) bloom in great abundance after rain, often growing to a height of three feet. They have flat seeds covered with white hairs. Facing page bottom: brittlebush (*Encelia farinosa*).

This plant is found in most of America's arid regions. Indians used to chew the stems, which exude a fragrant resin. Above: desert marigolds (*Baileya multiradiata*) and jumping, or teddybear, cholla (*Opuntia bigelovii*).

Below: Spanish daggers (*Yucca torreyi*) in bloom. These have rigid, sharp leaves which can cause severe injuries to men or horses and are pollinated by specialist yucca moths. Facing page: yucca growing beside ocotillo (*Fouquieria splendens*) in Arizona, and (overleaf) Joshua trees (*Yucca brevifolia*). These can form miniature forests in some areas. They were named by the Mormons, who thought the plants looked like men holding up their arms to God.

Lechuguilla (*Agave lecheguilla*) (above) has vicious leaves and was a dangerous obstacle for early explorers. Fibres for weaving were obtained from the leaves. Facing page: century plants (*Agave sp.*). Contrary to popular belief, these plants do not require a century before they flower, though they do take many years. They are pollinated by bats, some of which feed exclusively on the pollen and nectar of this plant.

These pages: barrel cactus (*Ferocactus wislizenii*). This large cactus, which can grow to a height of ten feet, is found across southern Arizona to western Texas and into northern Mexico. It has long, sharp spines growing in clusters on the ridges of its barrel. The stouter spines in the center are surrounded by thinner ones. In each cluster, one of the spines curves sharply downwards towards the tip, giving the plant the alternative name of "fishhook cactus." It flowers from April to May, bearing a ring of flowers at the top of the plant, and is used for making cactus candy.

Above: hedgehog cactus (*Echinocereus dasyacanthus*), and (facing page) another hedgehog cactus (*Echinocereus sp.*). Overleaf: strawberry cactus (*Echinocereus stramineus*). All the beautiful flowers of these cacti seem to be out of proportion to the main plant. Several similar species are found throughout the arid regions of America, but they can be difficult to identify as the growth form of the plants may vary considerably, along with the flower size and color. In good years a multitude of flowers can be produced, providing a spectacular display.

The largest of all cacti is the saguaro (*Cereus gigantea*) (these pages and overleaf), which can grow to fifty feet in height and live for up to 200 years. Its blossom is the state flower of Arizona, where it is protected by law because, in recent years, many plants have been collected illegally to supply a growing demand for ornamental cacti. The area is now patrolled in an effort to curb the trade. The saguaro cactus is a very important part of the desert ecosystem, housing owls and other birds in holes in its stem and providing copious quantities of nectar for bats, doves, moths and other insects.

Above: claret-cup cactus (*Echinocereus triglochidiatus*). This is one of the most popular and familiar of America's cacti, with its multitude of long-lasting scarlet flowers. It has a number of common names, including "king's cup cactus" and "strawberry cactus." It is found over a large part of the Southwest, from Colorado and New Mexico westwards to Arizona, Nevada and California. There are many local varieties and subspecies with different stem-growth forms as well as size and color variations of the flowers. Their spines vary too, both in number and size. They can be found in clusters of two or three very stout spines or up to fifteen thinner ones. Depending on the local conditions and prevailing weather, claret-cup cacti can be found in bloom from about April to July. Like many other cacti, this species has been extensively collected from the wild and has, unfortunately, become scarce in many areas. Accordingly, it is now protected in a large number of states. Left: bunch-ball cactus (*Echinocereus coccineus*), and (facing page) prickly pear cactus (*Opuntia sp.*) in the Sonoran Desert. The prickly pear is a complex genus of cacti. Most of them have flattened stems and, like most cacti, it can reproduce vegetatively, growing roots or shoots from any part of its structure, even from tiny fragments of stem. It can, therefore, multiply at an astonishing rate and has given rise to many problems in areas where it has been introduced, such as Australia.

The beavertail cactus (*Opuntia basilaris*) (these pages) is remarkable among opuntias in having no spines on the stem pads. Instead, quarter-inch-long bristles grow in clusters on the flower-bearing stems. Single flowers appear from March to June on top of cylindrical stems around the top edge of the main flat stem. It is generally a small plant, growing just twelve inches high, but does tend to grow in clumps up to six feet wide. Found in the drier parts of Utah and Arizona, southwards to the Sonoran Desert, its name comes from the resemblance of its flattened stems to the tail of a beaver. Overleaf: desert monkey flower (*Mimulus bigefoul*) in Anza-Borrego Desert State Park, California.